UNSUITABLE GIRLS

Dolly Dhingra

UNSUITABLE GIRLS

OBERON BOOKS

LONDON

First published in 2001 by Oberon Books Ltd.
(incorporating Absolute Classics)
521 Caledonian Road, London N7 9RH
Tel: 020 7607 3637 / Fax: 020 7607 3629
e-mail: oberon.books@btinternet.com

A catalogue record for this book is available from the British
Library.

ISBN: 1 84002 223 X

Cover design: Andrzej Klimowski

Typography: Richard Doust

Printed & bound by Antony Rowe Ltd, Eastbourne

Dedicated to
my Mum and Dad

Characters

(It is possible to perform this play with 3 female and
3 male actors)

The Girls

CHUMPA
Bossy heroine, 28

SAB
Chumpa's mate from childhood, 25

MANDY
Chumpa's mate from childhood, 28

MUM
Chumpa's mum, 55

AUDREY
Editor of *High Society*, in her 40s

MRS MIDDLETON
Personnel officer of Dodgy Publications Ltd

WOMAN
At dating agency

The Lads

ASHOK
Chumpa's boyfriend, 28

MEM
Ashok's cousin, 28

VINOD
Bollywood actor, 32

MANOJ
Ashok's father and local businessman

MR PATEL
Editor of *Concrete Weekly*

AGENT
Vinod's agent

ROBIN
A date

SUNIL
A date

JAG
A date

DOCTOR

DATES
A number of quick-fire lines from male actors

MAN
At Asian marriage agency

Unsuitable Girls was first performed at the Contact Theatre, Manchester, on 10 November 2000, with the following cast:

CHUMPA, Shelley Conn

SAB/MUM, Asha Kahlon

MANDY/MRS MIDDLETON/AUDREY,
   Naomi Thompson

ASHOK, Purvez Qadir

MEM/MR PATEL/ROBIN/DOCTOR,
   Gary Pillai

MANOJ/VINOD, Alex Khan

Other parts were played by members of the company

Director, Kully Thiarai

Assistant Directors, Ada Nzeribe/Alison Reed

Stage Manager, Lucy Edkins

Assistant Stage Manager, Rachel Candler

Lighting, David Martin

Sound, Greg Akehurst

The play embarked on a tour in the summer of 2001 with the Pilot Theatre Company, with the following cast:

CHUMPA, Manjinder Virk

SAB/MUM, Asha Kahlon

MANDY, Naomi Thompson

ASHOK, Antony Hickling

MEM, Ravi Ajula

MANOJ/VINOD, Royce Ullah

Other parts were played by members of the company

Director, Kully Thiarai

Movement Director, Faroque Khan

Musical Director, Jaydev Mistry

Production Manager, Gareth Williams

Set Designer, Keith Khan

Lighting Designer, James Farncombe

Technical Stage Manager, Louise Dancy

Set in the East End of London.

The present.

ACT ONE

Scene 1

CHUMPA is sitting on a bench in a swimming pool's changing room dressed in a Punjabi wedding outfit, crying her eyeballs out. It is relentless. Her mobile rings. She takes a deep breath, composes herself and then answers it.

CHUMPA: Mandy? I'm not telling you. Well, if you're my best friend you'd understand. I need to think, I'll call you.

She ends the call and immediately starts sobbing. The phone rings again. She composes herself.

I'm fine, really, Sab. I won't do anything stupid, I don't want to talk right now. I'm switching my phone off.

She clicks her mobile phone and immediately starts to sob. She undresses. Underneath her clothes she is wearing a swimming costume. She sobs as she talks.

Listen God, things got out of hand – there was just too much pressure. I can't marry him, I can't. It was Ashok's Dad's fault. He wouldn't stop going on about it – it started at my cousin's wedding. Remember?

Bhangra music overhead. MANOJ and MUM walk on.

MANOJ: What parent doesn't want their child to be married?

MUM: She has to be ready.

MANOJ: How's your health?

MUM: Pains in my chest are not going away.

She clutches her heart.

MANOJ: Must be worry, get her married and then your mind will be free. I promised your husband that I would take care of things. Since children they've known each other. All this girlfriend boyfriend nonsense – you like someone then get married, simple. Have children, work hard, die, end. That's life.

MUM: If her father were alive he could talk some sense to her. Is Ashok ready?

MANOJ: Of course. We've been getting offers from India. I said to him, 'be patient,' but a man can't wait forever.

MUM: Why doesn't he ask her?

MANOJ: No man would ask if he thinks he's going to get no for an answer. I'll talk to him. Ashok! Ashok!

He goes off to find ASHOK. He does so and the conversation continues without MUM being able to hear it.

MANOJ: Ask her now.

ASHOK: Ask who what?

MANOJ: Chumpa, marriage.

ASHOK: Oh Daaad we're at a wedding.

MANOJ: Exactly, and don't Daaad Waaad me. We need a woman. Five years, your mother's been gone and not one loving meal cooked in our house.

ASHOK: That's why takeaways were invented.

MANOJ stares at ASHOK – he is not amused.

MANOJ: A house is a cold place without a woman.

ASHOK: Turn the heating up then.

MANOJ: Shut up fool.

In the meantime CHUMPA has appeared and is talking to MUM. The two conversations between the couples are intercut.

MUM: Ashok's father's been asking.

CHUMPA: Branson? What's he want?

MUM: Don't call him that, he's a good businessman. Wants to talk to you – they're getting offers from India.

CHUMPA: Any idiot can get married – only have to sign a piece of paper.

MUM: He's serious, getting fed up cooking and cleaning himself.

CHUMPA: I don't want to be no full-time flippin' cleaner, I got an education.

MUM: Tut. It's called being a daughter-in-law.

CHUMPA: Slave more like.

MUM: We agreed, up to twenty-five you could do career, be journalist, joonalist whatever but then you would get married.

CHUMPA: It's not like I haven't been trying. They're not gonna give us their best jobs without putting up a fight you know.

MUM: No, I don't know. We agreed – three years overdue.

CHUMPA: Life doesn't work to a timetable – maybe God's got other things in store for me.

MUM: Everything works to a timetable, you won't be having children at fifty. You think I'll be alive then to look after them. What will happen to your carccr when you have to stay at home all day looking after children? I won't live forever.

MANOJ and ASHOK approach CHUMPA and MUM.

MANOJ: Chumpa dear. How are you beti?

CHUMPA: Fine, Uncle.

MANOJ: Don't call me Uncle any more.

CHUMPA: Why not, Uncle?

MANOJ: Ashok has something to ask you.

He nudges ASHOK.

ASHOK: Yeah, right, err…

CHUMPA looks uncomfortable and gives him an intense stare. MANOJ and MUM look hopeful.

Want a drink?

MANOJ forces a laugh and then gives ASHOK a stare.

MANOJ: Such a joker. Go on…

ASHOK: Let's dance.

He pulls her away from the parents.

MUM: Dance in front of the video-man.

ASHOK: That was close.

CHUMPA: Maybe we should just stop seeing each other…

ASHOK: Don't start, we're at a party.

CHUMPA sighs.

Some bhangra music begins.

MANOJ: Our children will be getting married next, come on let's dance.

A funky Bhangra number starts in which all take on the various roles to be found at a Punjabi wedding. Everyone's having a great time until MUM goes all weak and passes out.

CHUMPA: Stop! Stop! Somebody help. I said help!

The music stops and CHUMPA is in a hospital talking to a DOCTOR. A heartbeat machine bleeps overhead.

DOCTOR: It's extremely puzzling – there's no medical history of any previous heart problems. Was she under any mental or emotional pressure lately?

CHUMPA: I don't think so.

DOCTOR: Hmm. You know sometimes a person can lose the will to live if they feel they have nothing to live for, if they're unhappy – a kind of spiritual depression.

CHUMPA: She's got me to live for. She *is* happy. We've been going swimming regularly changed from ghee to olive oil, she's a lot healthier. She's not going to…? Is she?

DOCTOR: Your mum's an unusual case. I'll have to consult my colleagues. Why don't you use the time to…just in case…

The DOCTOR leaves.

CHUMPA: Oh God, please don't let Mum die. Not yet. It sounds selfish but I haven't achieved anything. You took Dad, at least let me make Mum proud. Patel said I can write my first article, he's promised. They always wanted a writer in the family.

The sound of the heartbeat machine stops beeping and there is the sound of a single tone to suggest death.

Mum, you can't leave me on my own. Said you wouldn't be at peace unless I was married. You waited all of your life for the day. God let my mum live to see me wed. I'll get married God I promise – let Mum live and I'll get married. Mum!!!

The death tone continues and CHUMPA bursts into tears and buries her face in her hands and sobs – as she does so an electrician walks in and fiddles around with the wires at the back of the heart machine. It starts bleeping regularly and he leaves. CHUMPA looks up and is stunned. She looks around as if for an explanation. She wipes her tears.

Oh, thank you God. Thank you. I'll get married. I promise.

The DOCTOR walks over. CHUMPA smiles at him wiping away the tears.

Doctor, there is a god, there is!

DOCTOR: Who can say? I'm sorry if it gave you a fright. As I suspected it's just a minor case of heartburn. Keep her off spicy foods for a while.

CHUMPA: Thank you.

She hugs the DOCTOR, who is stunned.

Scene 2

MUM and MANOJ are sitting together. MANOJ pulls a piece of paper from out of his pocket.

MANOJ: From Guruji, wedding on the thirteenth of August – a truly auspicious day for a wedding. Says that it is Chumpa's destiny to marry into our family.

MUM: Ha! Only four months away! No time to waste. I'll go to Delhi, invite relatives.

MANOJ: Go before the end of next week, prices are still low. How are you for money?

MUM: A lot of people we have to invite.

MANOJ: Let us not worry about the dowry doory too much. The cost of the wedding is yours. You understand?

MUM wrings her hands.

MUM: Of course we must stick to some tradition.

MANOJ delves into his inside jacket pocket and produces three bundles of cash and puts them down on the table.

MANOJ: Take this for India. Buy Chumpa whatever she needs. Gold from your uncle, saris from Tilk Nagar. Will you go to Punjab or just Delhi?

MUM: I'll go to the Golden Temple.

MANOJ: Yes, get blessings all around. I'll sort out an internal flight.

MUM looks a bit hesitant for a moment.

MUM: …Just one thing she asked for……she said that she doesn't want to live…

She looks awkward.

MANOJ: Yes, yes, I know, they are young, they want independence. They don't want to live with me? Fine.

MUM is surprised.

MUM: You hundred per cent sure?

MANOJ: Of course. They can live next door above my video shop.

Scene 3

CHUMPA and MANDY in a homely space, looking through some glossy magazines.

MANDY: It's all a bit sudden that's all I'm saying.

CHUMPA: Everyone gets married, so I might as well get it over and done with.

MANDY: You're a real romantic – anyone ever tell you that?

CHUMPA: You married for love and look what happened.

MANDY: So you're admitting it's not for love then?

CHUMPA: I didn't say that.

MANDY: You didn't say you didn't either.

CHUMPA: Oh stop giving me a hard time.

SAB enters all excited.

SAB: Thirteenth of August! Your mum told me. Congratulations.

She gives CHUMPA a big hug. SAB starts singing.

Going to the temple and we're gonna get married, going to the temple and we're gonna get married. So what hall? How many people? DJ or Band? Honeymoon plans? What colour outfit, pink? Red?

CHUMPA: Not now, I'm off to work. I'll tell you all about it this evening. See you later.

SAB: Ahhhhh.

CHUMPA gives SAB a hug.

It's so exciting. I want to know every detail.

CHUMPA: Yes, yes alright. See ya later Mand.

MANDY: Yeah laters.

CHUMPA leaves.

I can't understand why she didn't discuss it.

SAB: You can discuss things to death.

MANDY: Never heard her say a good thing about marriage.

SAB: Some marriages do work out.

MANDY: Not many.

SAB: I said some.

MANDY: Just 'cause you make the finishing line don't mean you're happy.

SAB: Well what would you want for her? Give her space to make her own mistakes.

MANDY: Mistakes hurt.

SAB: I can tell. How much longer for the divorce?

MANDY: Not supposed to use the D word. Six months and then I'm off to Brazil.

SAB: You haven't seen culture until you've been to a Punjabi wedding, they're totally mad. Carnival meets care in the community all at once. You'll have to wear Indian clothes. I know this great woman who does henna, this model in Asian Bride had it done down the side of her leg, very sexy, I'm thinking about it.

MANDY: Why the hurry though?

SAB: He's a bit charmless for my liking, but still, each to their own. They've been going out long enough. Who wants to be single anyway?

MANDY: Married people.

SAB: We should be happy for her. I've had an idea for the hen night – there's this massive salsa ball the night before the wedding.

MANDY: Sounds alright, we better get practising.

SAB gets up to demonstrate and the two dance together for a while.

Scene 4

CHUMPA is at work typing, looking totally bored out of her mind. Overhead we hear the ticking of an austere clock.

She reads what she has typed.

'Dear Mr Patel, not so much a suicide note but more a death by boredom note. I'm dying here.'

Totally bored she switches the radio on and twiddles the dial. She stops at a station and begins to listen to an interviewer.

RADIO VOICE/ INTERVIEWER: After having made a hundred and thirty-two Bollywood movies – what does an actor of your calibre do next?

RADIO VOICE/VINOD: Life's horizon does not get any closer. As an actor I'm on a journey like any other mortal soul. I do not worry about tomorrow, God has brought me this far and I trust him to take me to where I need to get to.

RADIO VOICE/INTERVIEWER: I understand you are a great lover of London. How long are you here for this time?

RADIO VOICE/VINOD: Not long enough, I come to London as much as I can. I can't keep away. My show's on at the Palladium for the next three months. After that who knows which way the winds of creativity will blow.

RADIO VOICE/INTERVIEWER: And what about other future plans? I understand you are still single.

RADIO VOICE/VINOD: Yes, I'm afraid very much so, but I hope not to be for too long. I'm looking to settle down, I think I have reached that juncture in life and I am looking forward to commitment and growing with another being.

RADIO VOICE/INTERVIEWER: Who is she?

RADIO VOICE/VINOD: That I'm afraid remains to be seen.

RADIO VOICE/INTERVIEWER: And, of course, you are up for the part of Hamlet at the National Theatre.

RADIO VOICE/VINOD: Yes.

RADIO VOICE/INTERVIEWER: It would be a first for an Asian actor.

RADIO VOICE/VINOD: Yes.

RADIO VOICE/INTERVIEWER: But there are some difficulties.

RADIO VOICE/VINOD: Yes, technical but I am sure we will be able to iron those out, even though I hate ironing.

Some phoney laughter by both voices.

RADIO VOICE/INTERVIEWER: Vinod Kumar it's been a pleasure talking to you.

RADIO VOICE/VINOD: Not at all, the pleasure was all mine. Thank you.

RADIO VOICE/INTERVIEWER: And the next record you've selected is one of your all-time favourites.

A song plays and CHUMPA gets completely lost in it. We see VINOD dancing like the star he is, with women around him. As the song comes to an end ASHOK appears and taps a number into his mobile. The phone on CHUMPA's desk rings. Lost in her dream she doesn't hear it. MR PATEL has now appeared and is watching her from a distance. She does not notice him. CHUMPA hears the phone, turns the music down and the dancers disappear.

CHUMPA: *Concrete Weekly* editor's office. Ashok, hi, what do you want?

ASHOK: I've been ringing for ages, where were you?

CHUMPA: I was busy.

ASHOK: Hurry up, I'm waiting outside. I need a favour.

CHUMPA: I can't just clock off ten minutes early. Not all of us work for our family. Some of us have proper careers.

ASHOK: It's hardly a job, let alone a career.

CHUMPA: Mr Patel wants me to be a journalist.

ASHOK: That man's a sap. He hates Punjabis. And he's tight.

CHUMPA looks around the room and spots MR PATEL. She snaps into action animatedly.

CHUMPA: Mr Williams, I'll alert one of our journalists right away. No, it's no trouble at all.

ASHOK: Who's Mr Williams?

MR PATEL starts making his way over.

CHUMPA: Mr Patel's coming over.

ASHOK: What you on about?

MR PATEL leans over to grab the phone from CHUMPA's hand but she puts her hand over it.

CHUMPA: (*To MR PATEL.*) Says it's confidential – I'll transfer it to your office.

ASHOK: I don't want to speak to him.

MR PATEL looks puzzled and begins to walk towards his supposed office.

CHUMPA: (*Into phone.*) You've got a call waiting?

ASHOK: You're a bloody nutcase. I'm outside and hurry up.

He shakes his head in dismay. MR PATEL turns around and bounds towards CHUMPA's desk and attempts to get the phone off of her.

CHUMPA: (*Quickly.*) You'll call him back? Right, very good Mr Williams. Goodbye.

She puts the phone down. MR PATEL looks exasperated and ASHOK walks off shaking his head.

MR PATEL: You think I'm a donkey? You think you can take the pissy out of me?

CHUMPA: I beg your pardon?

MR PATEL: Yes, yes, beg – beg all you like young lady. You think you are so clever? But you are not. You are stupid – that it why you are the secretary and me editor.

CHUMPA: Which reminds me Mr Patel, you said that I could write my first piece this week.

MR PATEL: You can't even answer the phone properly.

CHUMPA: That's all I ever do. It's been almost two years.

MR PATEL: Is that how long I have been paying you? Good-for-nothing.

CHUMPA gets ready to leave.

CHUMPA: Look Mr Patel, the deal was that I'd work as your secretary for a year and then I'd get promoted to writing. You promised.

MR PATEL: A girl of your age should be married. Get married to that good-for-nothing Punjabi Ashok then you can both be good-for-nothing Punjabis together – have good-for-nothing Punjabi children and they can give you good-for-nothing Punjabi grandchildren.

CHUMPA: I'd love to continue this great philosophical debate but I'm heading off. I am getting married but it won't stop me from pursuing my writing career. See ya.

MR PATEL: Stupid Punjabi girl.

He slams his fist down on the desk.

CHUMPA leaves and finds ASHOK waiting for her.

ASHOK: Took your time. What was all that about?

CHUMPA: Nothing. What's up?

ASHOK: You gotta drive me to the airport tomorrow. I've got to collect my cousin.

CHUMPA: You asking or telling me?

ASHOK: Asking. Pretty please.

CHUMPA: Thought you said you'd rather use public transport than have me drive. Where's your car?

ASHOK: Don't give me a hard time right, I had an accident driving back from Jagi's last night.

CHUMPA: Your Dad's car?

ASHOK: Mate's BMW ZX. Silver, beautiful, real shame.

CHUMPA: Borrow mine, I'm off to see the girls.

ASHOK: They're a waste of space.

CHUMPA: Oh shut up.

ASHOK becomes sheepish.

ASHOK: I can't drive. I was over the limit.

CHUMPA: Drink driving!? How many times have I told you. Was anyone hurt?

ASHOK: No. I hit the curb and went flying into Forest Gate police station. What shit luck.

CHUMPA is shaking her head.

CHUMPA: Jesus Christ. Suppose you were smoking a joint at the time as well?

ASHOK: Luckily we'd finished puffing the gear at Jagi's.

CHUMPA: God you're so thick. You make me so angry, just leave me alone for a while right.

She storms off and ASHOK goes after her.

ASHOK: Don't be like that.

Scene 5

CHUMPA walks into a homely space where the girls are.

SAB: Here she is. I've got something for you. I should give it to both of you, it's an engagement card.

MANDY: Where is Ashok these days? Haven't seen him for ages.

SAB: I saw him walking down Green Street on Saturday with Sangeeta.

MANDY: Sangeeta's got legs?

SAB: Yep, saw 'em with my own eyes.

MANDY: Thought she was glued into that flash car of hers.

SAB: Heard she had an accident.

CHUMPA: When?

SAB: Last night, the girls at work told me.

CHUMPA: What's she drive?

SAB: ZX BMW. Silver. Nice car.

MANDY: That girl's so thick.

SAB: And a slapper. Her brother's really nice, wouldn't mind marrying him. What's it like being out of the singles zone at last Chumps?

MANDY: Look at that face. Can't you tell she's over the moon?

CHUMPA: Help me do a wedding list – that is the best thing isn't it?

SAB: I'd say.

MANDY: Definitely. Otherwise you'll have half a dozen ironing boards on your hands.

CHUMPA: Shall I ask for money?

MANDY: People like giving gifts.

SAB: Indians give really crap gifts. Make a wedding list otherwise you'll spend the rest of your life giving 'em away to other people getting married. It's a real headache cos you got to make sure you don't give them back to the family that gave 'em to you. My Mum was always doing that. The rows it led to.

MANDY: Do you love him?

SAB: She's getting married. Give it a couple of months and they'll be farting in each other's company. When exactly are you allowed to fart in front of one another?

CHUMPA: Never.

MANDY: When the farting starts the honeymoon's over. Graham would fart in bed and then put the duvet over my head. I read it as a sign.

MANDY: So, do you love him?

SAB: It's different in our culture. They say you learn to love one another.

MANDY: And if you don't?

SAB: Then you've got the kids and other members of the family to love. We don't exactly sit at home watching TV with our husbands for the rest of our lives. There're other things.

MANDY: What, like Ashok's father for instance?

SAB: For instance. Now, have we decided on the salsa ball for hen night? 'Cause I'll need to book tickets.

CHUMPA/MANDY: Yeah.

MANDY: Ask for what you want – you only live once and if you're really lucky you only marry once.

CHUMPA: Getting divorced, what was it like?

SAB: Can we not go there please?

MANDY: I think we should. You want to know? It was fucking shit.

SAB: Time to get morbid.

There is a pregnant pause for a while.

MANDY: People rush into marriage. I did. Like it's going to save them from themselves. Even when I was saying my vows I knew deep down it was a lie. I wish someone had taught me to listen to my instincts – that's all anyone's got. When he left me it was like being in an abyss that I'd never get out of. Felt like the sky was black for the longest time. Didn't smile for about two years – thought I never would.

SAB: Would you ever get married again?

MANDY: No one ever died of being single.

CHUMPA: Do you ever get scared?

SAB: Scared?

MANDY: Of what?

CHUMPA: I don't know – of everything, of the future, of life. I mean what if you're destined never to be happy? What if you never find it?

MANDY: It? You mean love?

CHUMPA: No. The reason we're here? What life's really about.

SAB: You'll freak yourself out – you think too much.

MANDY: Most people don't think like that. They plod along, no questions asked, go to work, go down the pub, watch telly – life's alright.

SAB: Millions of years of evolution just to watch telly?

CHUMPA: But what about dreams? Ambitions?

MANDY: Everyone has dreams, but you have to make a choice – go for 'em or bury 'em. Turning dreams into reality is a slog – most people can't be arsed. I'm gonna travel the world, that's my dream. Oh, and don't expect people to like you for following your dreams, most of them will hate you for it. Reminds them that they killed their own. You know you'll never be a writer if you marry Ashok…

There is a pause. SAB sees something desirable in one of the catalogues.

SAB: Ah, you've got to get this foot spa.

Some wedding music.

Scene 6

Overhead some airport sounds. ASHOK walks on in a hurry, CHUMPA trails behind. She clicks a car alarm on.

VOICE ON TANNOY: Flight Air India flight 438L has been delayed by three hours.

ASHOK: Come on, hurry up, we're late. Told you to take the A406. How many times I told you that you've gotta learn to park better than that? It's embarrassing.

CHUMPA: Yeah, well if you hadn't been so bloody stupid drinking and driving you could park your own penis extension.

ASHOK: Women talk such crap.

CHUMPA: What flight was he supposed to be on? How's he related to you?

ASHOK: Some kind of cousin. Never met him. Lives in America. Dad thought it would be good for him to come to the wedding. He got ditched recently. Girl ran off with his best mate. Went to India to find himself.

CHUMPA: He should've just looked in the mirror.

ASHOK: You're not funny you know.

CHUMPA: Yeah and you're hilarious.

ASHOK: Ah shut up.

CHUMPA: Shut up yourself.

ASHOK: You're getting on my nerves.

CHUMPA: I asked what flight?

ASHOK: Don't boss me around right.

CHUMPA: I asked – asked ain't bossing.

ASHOK reluctantly pulls out a piece of paper from his trouser pocket – making a bit of a show of it.

VOICE ON TANNOY: Flight Air India flight 438FL has been delayed by three hours.

ASHOK: Bingo. Looks like we'll just have to sit down the pub.

CHUMPA: So you can get shit-faced while I'm chauffeur and entertainer to your stupid cousin? I don't think so.

ASHOK: Well what do you suggest?

CHUMPA: I'm gonna be late for work. Bring him on the train.

ASHOK: Public transport! What kind of impression is that to make on someone? Be reasonable.

CHUMPA: Reasonable? You drive into a police station drunk and now you want to sit on your fat arse down the pub. Is there nothing else to do in the world but get pissed? Is your greatest achievement how many pints you can drink without falling over? Is that as big as your ambition gets, Ashok?

ASHOK: Ambition? What you talking about? It was a couple of pints, having a bit of a laugh. You're enough to drive a man to drink – always moaning about something.

CHUMPA: Would you rather I burst into applause?

ASHOK: My mates are right about you. They reckon you're really miserable, really dissatisfied.

CHUMPA: Oh right yeah, your mates. Fools satisfied – the lot of them. You hang around with some ropy guys. They're pretty low down on the evolutionary scale – we're talking pond life, at best, mud people.

ASHOK: At least I've got friends.

CHUMPA: With friends like yours you don't need pets.

ASHOK: You know your problem?

CHUMPA: I bet I'm about to find out.

ASHOK: You're so wrapped up in…? In? In? What are you wrapped up in Chumpa? Because, you know what? I don't know, you know, and I'd really like to. You carry on as if you're a cut above the rest and all you are is a stupid secretary at a stupid newspaper and if you think that Mr Patel's gonna let you be a journalist you're a mug.

CHUMPA: Yes he is.

ASHOK: No he's not.

CHUMPA: Yes he is.

ASHOK: No he's not. Cos you can't write for shit.

CHUMPA stares at him and there is a very tense silence in which ASHOK understands he's overstepped the mark.

At least I'm happy Chumpa – that counts for something.

CHUMPA is seething.

CHUMPA: Oh yeah, what you happy about? You never followed any of your dreams, working at your Dad's travel agent, when was that part of the big plan? Because you know what? I don't remember. What happened to your music career? What happened to us travelling? What happened to us moving out of the flippin' East End? The video shop next door to your dad and opposite my mum's. We've lived on that street since the year dot. I haven't been further than flippin' Calais since the fifth form. What's happened to our lives?

ASHOK: We're supposed to be getting married.

There is a pregnant pause for a while.

CHUMPA: Supposed to be, Ashok.

ASHOK: What's that mean? It was your big idea.

CHUMPA: My idea? Branson's the one who keeps bugging my mum about it.

ASHOK: Told you not to call him that. Have some respect.

CHUMPA: You're a fine one to talk about respect. If you didn't want to get married why didn't you say so? Suppose you only said yes so you and your mates could get pissed without paying for a round.

ASHOK: Well why else would a guy wanna marry you?

There is silence.

CHUMPA: Can't thing of any reason why a girl would want to marry you.

They stand uncomfortably at what hangs between them. CHUMPA throws the car keys at him and storms off. There are a few airport sounds as ASHOK stands there. As she stomps to work she talks to God.

What a wanker. I can't marry a wanker, God. I couldn't stand being more miserable than I already am. Thought Mum was dying. Don't know if the promise counts for flippin' heartburn. Thought it was a heart attack. And that bloody shitbag Patel, he had better have some good news for me, right.

She looks at her watch, sighs.

Scene 7

She walks into her office to be met by MRS MIDDLETON waiting for her at her desk.

MRS MIDDLETON: Ah Chumpa Chameli you're late, again. I'm Kate Middleton, the personnel manager, Mr Patel suggested we speak. Now, I'm fully aware that you may not consider *Concrete Weekly* to be the most important publication in the world, but to our clients concrete is their life blood. They do not expect their interest in concrete to be ridiculed. You are the front line of the business. Saying, 'awesome' or 'hold the front page' when reporters phone in stories from the Congress of Hydraulic Cement Concrete production is neither funny nor clever. Your line manager suggests that you are flippant and unhelpful and that you show a persistent unwillingness to learn or to take criticism. *Concrete Weekly* no longer requires your services.

CHUMPA: You can't sack me. Patel promised I could try my hand at journalism – that's why…

MRS MIDDLETON: *Mr* Patel. We are not sacking you. This company's commitment to equal opportunities is not mere window dressing young lady. I circulated your details and we've managed to get you an offer, she wants to see you first though. Ms Sackville, she's on the Thirteenth floor, Unit 5b.

CHUMPA: I want to write.

MRS MIDDLETON: Beggars can't be choosers and it's not as if you have any experience. She's waiting.

She walks back seemingly into another office.

CHUMPA: I've come to see Ms Sackville.

AUDREY: About time. Are you Chumpa?

CHUMPA nods.

Audrey Sackville, editor of *High Society*. Being fired from *Concrete Weekly* is some achievement. You must be a real pain in the arse.

CHUMPA: Err…

AUDREY: Rhetorical question darling. Mr Patel says you have no drive.

CHUMPA: I've got a front garden though.

AUDREY: Oh very droll. You will not be late again. We start at nine-thirty and work as late as we have to. We always meet our deadlines. It's just the two of us producing the magazine single handedly for the numbskulls and cheapskates who happen to be our employers. Fortunately sixty per cent of the work consists of retyping press releases and reader's problems, neither of which are in short supply. You missing *Concrete Weekly* yet?

CHUMPA shakes her head.

I have to warn you – for me this is a temporary assignment. I'm waiting to hear from *Cosmo* – they'll want me as their features editor no doubt, once what's-her-face drops her sprog. Glossy magazines are my forte. In the meantime a woman's got to pay the mortgage somehow. What's your typing speed?

CHUMPA: Sixty words per minute.

AUDREY: Shorthand?

CHUMPA: Sorry.

AUDREY: Word?

CHUMPA: Yep.

AUDREY: Any knowledge of Indian cinema?

CHUMPA: Loads.

AUDREY: Good. We've got to list all those Bollywood films, include the Asian channels in our TV guide. Mulicultural society and all, brown being the new grey. I can never get the spellings right. I'm open to ideas, suggestions. You'll have to muck in and it's a slog. Want the job?

CHUMPA: What are the writing prospects like?

AUDREY: Prospects? Why, you'll have to be creative in every respect. Ever tried writing the listings for three hundred and seventy-five episodes of the Mahabarat? You'll be doing the event guide, horoscopes, recipes. We'll be making it up as we go along. Yes or a no?

CHUMPA: Definitely a yes.

AUDREY claps her hands.

AUDREY: First issue in a month – interview with Jemima Khan as our lead – let's get cracking.

Scene 8

CHUMPA is in the swimming pool changing rooms.

CHUMPA: Thanks for the job, God. Audrey's a bit mad. Nice though – she'll let me write.

Her mobile phone rings.

Hello? No Ashok's not with me. Who is it? Hello? I said who are you?

The person on the other end hangs up.

Why'd you keep ringing this number?

She dials 1471 to find out who it is.

Number withheld. It's Sangeeta, I bet it is. God, I've been meaning to talk to you about the Ashok thing. He hasn't been round, hasn't called – can't be arsed.

The phone rings again and she lets it for a while and then picks it up.

Piss off! Mum? No everything is fine. You don't need to shout. Ashok? He's fine too. Shoe size? Five. You confirmed your flight back? No Ashok won't – I'll pick you up from the airport. How's your health? We're all excited. Yes, okay, bye.

She puts the phone down.

Shit.

She sits there thinking for a while.

Yeah, right where was I? I know I said I'd get married but I think I was conned, not by you personally but events. Legally speaking a deal isn't a deal unless it's offer and acceptance and I didn't hear you accept.

She stops for a moment.

I'm not retracting – all I'm saying is that, that… What am I saying?

She does some stretching and then some deep breathing.

When in doubt meditate.

She sits down and meditates for a moment and assumes the position and closes her eyes for a short while. She has a brilliant idea and opens her eyes in amazement.

Hey you know what? If I remember correctly I said that I'd get married – I didn't say to Ashok. God, this shit really works, excellent.

She is amazed at herself. She picks up the phone.

Hello? Sab? Where are you? I'll meet you at home in five minutes. Emotional emergency. Is Mandy with you? Hurry.

She puts the phone down and then paces around practising what she is going to say to her mates when they arrive. She adopts different tones for each sentence.

Look girls I fucked up...... Ashok doesn't love me...... It was a mistake...... The thing is, I'm crap.

Scene 9

At home. MANDY and SAB arrive out of breath.

MANDY/SAB: We ran.

MANDY: What's the matter?

They look at CHUMPA for an answer and CHUMPA falls silent.

SAB: What's going on?

They look at her expectantly there is silence for a while.

CHUMPA: I can't marry Ashok.

MANDY and SAB are stunned.

MANDY: Oh my God.

SAB: Shit.

CHUMPA begins to pace around. MANDY and SAB look at each other.

MANDY: Have you told your Mum?

CHUMPA: Course not.

MANDY: You've got to cancel.

CHUMPA: I can't, half of India will be descending on us in a month.

SAB: Twenty-four carat besti [shame], a lot of shame coming this way.

MANDY: Why did you ever say yes?

SAB: Let's not go there, it's not helpful. You absolutely sure?

CHUMPA: Course.

MANDY: You said that when you agreed to it.

CHUMPA: It was a mistake, I'm human – I'm allowed to make a mistake aren't I?

SAB: Couldn't you have made a different one?

MANDY: Well, better now than later.

CHUMPA: I'll have to find someone else.

MANDY: What?

SAB: Who?

CHUMPA: Another bloke. I can't cancel – Mum's borrowed loads of money from Ashok's Dad. I've thought about it, I've got to get married someday, it might as well be now.

MANDY: You haven't found a bloke in twenty-eight years, what makes you think you'll find him…

SAB: In fifty-three days?

CHUMPA: It's worth a try, what else can I do? I made a promise.

MANDY: Promises can be broken.

CHUMPA: I promised on my mother's life. There's a world out there.

SAB: What a mess.

MANDY: I can't believe you asked him to marry you in the first place.

SAB: She didn't.

MANDY: He asked?

CHUMPA: No.

MANDY: Am I missing something?

CHUMPA: His father asked my mother on his behalf to ask me.

MANDY: What?

SAB: You wouldn't understand – it works differently with Indians.

MANDY: Indians! Bloody Indians, I've got a lot of respect for your culture most of the time but you've got some weird ways. Did it occur to your parents for one moment that you two might not want to get married?

SAB: Our parents don't think that giving children too much choice is a good thing.

CHUMPA: Help me find my soul-mate.

MANDY: Not just a man, but a soul-mate! I'd find one myself if I knew how.

SAB: Get a copy of *Eastern Eye* – lonely hearts, we might as well get started.

CHUMPA: Right, back in a second.

SAB: There'll be a wedding yet.

She runs into the video shop.

CHUMPA: Rajo? Rajo? I need *Eastern Eye*, quickly. Where are you?

She looks around on the shelf for a newspaper but there are none there. There is a copy of 'Eastern Eye' on the counter which is opened up. CHUMPA folds it and steals it. MEM clears his throat and CHUMPA starts and pretends to look at some videos, finds one she likes and then puts it on the counter.

Oh? Where's Rajo?

MEM: He left. I'm his replacement. You taking this out?

CHUMPA: Yeah. My number's one-five-six-oh.

MEM searches for her card.

MEM: You've already got overdue videos out on this card – you'll have to pay your fines.

CHUMPA: I don't get fined.

MEM: You don't? Why's that?

CHUMPA: Rajo didn't used to fine me because, well because, he was my mate and more importantly the owner is Ashok's father.

MEM: I know he's Ashok's father. What's that got to do with anything?

CHUMPA: Well Ashok, right. I'm supposed to be erm… well was getting… Supposed to be, was getting better at bringing them back, the videos and err… Rajo sometimes used to let me off because he knows how hectic it can be for me because I'm a journalist you see and what with deadlines and err… How much are the fines?

MEM: Journalist? Twelve pounds fifty.

CHUMPA: Let me take this out and I'll promise to clear my account when I come in next.

MEM looks at the video she has chosen.

MEM: *Women on the Verge of a Nervous Breakdown?* I can't let you have that.

CHUMPA: Why is it crap?

MEM: No, because my employer says I can't issue further rentals on any account that's in debt. New policy.

CHUMPA: But I haven't got twelve pounds fifty on me.

MEM: I'm sorry to hear that, but that's not my problem.

CHUMPA: I've been coming to this video shop all my life.

MEM: For good reason, we do have the largest selection of titles north of the river in London.

CHUMPA: I don't need the sales pitch.

MEM: It's a fact.

CHUMPA: More than Blockbusters?

MEM: Including the Hindi titles, yes.

CHUMPA: Most of them are pirates and you have to squint to make out who the hero is.

MEM: I'm not getting into technicalities. How will you be paying?

CHUMPA: Oh, come on don't give me grief.

MEM: Grief is part of life. It's my second day on the job and I really wouldn't want to break any rules.

CHUMPA: What a job's worth. Where did they get you from? No, don't answer that, don't think I want to know. I'll pay tomorrow.

She begins to stomp off.

MEM: I'd like my paper back please.

CHUMPA stops in her tracks.

CHUMPA: Sorry?

MEM: My paper.

CHUMPA cannot believe what she is hearing. She is mortified.

I believe it's called theft.

CHUMPA is totally embarrassed but is trying to style it out.

You know you could just buy it, I was only reading the film reviews.

CHUMPA desperately fishes through her pockets and finds some coins. She slams them down on the counter.

CHUMPA: Right, I will. There you go.

She takes the paper and walks off.

MEM: Your change.

CHUMPA: Shove it up your arse.

She walks back to the girls.

This is all I could get.

They huddle round.

MANDY: This is bloody ridiculous.

SAB: Shut up, start looking.

CHUMPA: Audrey says nothing gets done without a deadline.

MANDY: She might have been referring to work.

Silently the three of them look at the adverts.

'A nice man from the midlands.' I didn't know there were any nice men in the midlands.

SAB: Here, 'Asian babe wanted for hot tandoori nights by tall dark prince in leather armour.'

MANDY: Catarrhing Sikh.

She makes some guttural sounds.

SAB: Kuthari Sikh you idiot.

CHUMPA: Be serious, how many you got?

MANDY: Two and a maybe.

CHUMPA: Maybes are nos. Sab?

SAB: Three, a couple for myself. You?

CHUMPA: None.

MANDY: What about a white bloke?

CHUMPA: They'd be asking me stupid questions all the time. 'Why d'you wear dots on your head? How do they get those rings through their nose?

SAB: Here. 'Artistic handsome Asian man, thirty, ready to settle down, seeks British Asian woman for passport to happiness.'

CHUMPA: Ideal.

MANDY: If this is going to work you'll have to try everything.

SAB: Register with dating agencies – I went to a couple of those, what an experience.

CHUMPA: Why?

Scene 10

MAN: Welcome to the Amazing Asian Marriage Bureau. Take a seat. I just need to ask you a few simple questions. Height?

CHUMPA: Medium.

MAN: Colour of eyes?

CHUMPA: Brown.

MAN: Complexion?

CHUMPA: Medium brown.

MAN looks up.

MAN: You mean dark.

CHUMPA: I'm not dark.

MAN: Actually, very dark.

CHUMPA: I'm not very dark.

MAN: Listen child we have a colour chart. It is standardised worldwide and absolutely definitive and according to that you are very dark. Disabilities?

CHUMPA: None.

MAN: None visible. Size?

CHUMPA: A bit overweight.

MAN: Thin.

CHUMPA: Definitely not thin.

MAN: Listen dear, despite the anorexic trends of the West, Indian men like their women plump. It gives us something to hold on to. How will you be paying?

CHUMPA: Cheque.

MAN: We are Indians and prefer cash.

A WOMAN appears.

WOMAN: I'm delighted you selected Destined Dates Miss Chameli. We're so pleased to have you on our books.

We get a lot of call for dusky maidens, especially from our older clients.

SAB: See everyone. Keep your options open and select the best of the bunch. If there are any.

MANDY: Nobody said it was going to be easy.

CHUMPA is introduced to an array of different male characters who say their lines and are off. The girls consider all of them and make faces at their inappropriateness.

DATE 1: Bill waiter. I really think we should meet again. Oh damn. Look can you get this? I'm all for women's lib.

DATE 2: Drugs? Well, no nothing heavy, just recreational stuff, puff some herbs, a line of Charlie now and again, an E at the weekends – just the usual.

DATE 3: Your eyes are like olives and your skin like almonds.

DATE 4: We'd have to live with my family. There's my five brothers and their wives, six nieces and nephews. We've got a big house – plenty of space for everyone.

DATE 5: I've never been married, never found the right girl. I've got three kids. Love 'em to bits.

DATE 6: I don't mind career women at all. You can work where you like, as long as I get three hot meals a day I'm happy.

CHUMPA: (*To SAB.*) God.

SAB: Gotta kiss a lot of frogs before you find a prince.

CHUMPA: That bloke stood me up, hasn't returned my calls.

SAB: Which one?

CHUMPA pulls out a piece of paper from her pocket.

CHUMPA: 'Artistic handsome Asian man, thirty, ready to settle down, seeks British Asian woman for passport to happiness.'

MANDY: Stuff him. His loss.

CHUMPA: What time we heading off this evening?

SAB: Nineish. We'll come over to yours.

CHUMPA: Right.

SAB and MANDY walk off.

MEM appears and CHUMPA is looking the other way and bumps into him.

CHUMPA/MEM: Sorry. Oh.

CHUMPA: Oh it's jobsworth. How are you?

MEM: That's not my name.

CHUMPA: You'd know.

MEM: Know what?

CHUMPA: Why Indian men are so crap?

MEM: I'm one. In case you hadn't noticed.

CHUMPA: I tell ya in the last two weeks I've met more low life than Jacques Cousteau.

MEM: It isn't low if it's water – it's deep.

CHUMPA: I beg your pardon?

MEM: You said more low life than Jacques Cousteau. He was a diver he didn't deal with low life, he dealt with sea life – the sea isn't low it's deep.

CHUMPA is astounded at his pedantry.

CHUMPA: You a trainspotter by any chance?

MEM: No. You were saying, about low life?

CHUMPA: I've got to get married.

MEM: Got to?

CHUMPA: Believe me I wouldn't be doing it otherwise.

MEM looks at her puzzled.

MEM: Well, you know what they say – 'Every blind alley helps you find the right road.'

CHUMPA: Quote me no quotes.

MEM: I was expecting to see you in the shop.

CHUMPA: You were?

MEM: Yes. Your fines amount to fourteen pounds and fifty pence.

CHUMPA looks a bit disappointed.

CHUMPA: The things Indians do to make money.

MEM: It goes to charity.

CHUMPA: Closet hippy are you?

MEM: I'm not a hippy. I'm an Indian. You know if you don't pay, the fines double each day.

CHUMPA: Jesus, is that what you do all day, plot ways to rip your customers off?

MEM: No.

CHUMPA: You want to get out a bit more often. Anyway can't stand here gasing to you all day I've got to dash…

MEM: What? Off to see more prospectives?

CHUMPA: No. I'm on the job, covering a story.

MEM: What on a Saturday night?

CHUMPA: Better than sitting in a video shop on your own.

MEM: You'd be surprised, some of my customers are remarkably interesting.

CHUMPA doesn't know what to make of his remark.

Come in soon – to clear those fines.

CHUMPA: Don't worry.

MEM: I don't.

They part. CHUMPA looks back at him. MEM heads straight off. CHUMPA gets together with the girls.

CHUMPA and SAB go through her wardrobe and begin to get dressed to party.

CHUMPA: Who we meeting?

SAB: They're friends of my cousins.

CHUMPA: Not the ones in Birmingham?

SAB: Nothing wrong with Brummies.

MANDY: Lot wrong with your cousins though.

They head out. Disco lights flash.

SAB: (*To MANDY.*) We'll let her have first pick.

MANDY: Her need is greater.

A guy shuffles over.

SUNIL: Hi, I'm Sunil. I'm sensual, sensitive and sexy and I'm going to show you special babes a super time. Let me buy you a drink.

SAB: Malibu and coke.

MANDY: Sweet cider.

CHUMPA: Orange juice.

SUNIL: You want something a bit stronger?

CHUMPA: I don't drink.

SUNIL: That is very sad.

He shuffles over to the bar.

SAB: What do you reckon?

CHUMPA: Why do guys with fat arses wear tight trousers? Do they think we like it or something?

SAB: I think he's cute.

MANDY: He's a prat.

Another bloke appears.

JAG: Hi, I'm Jag. I'm a driving instructor and under my bonnet I've got two litres of pure, smooth power. Let's go for a whirl on the dancefloor girls.

MANDY: He's alright.

SAB: I love this track, come on let's dance.

A modern day dance number, everyone dances.

The dance ends with them outside CHUMPA's house. Both SAB and MANDY have got lucky, CHUMPA has not. MANDY is arm-in-arm with a guy.

MANDY: We're off home. Goodnight.

They leave.

SAB: (*To CHUMPA.*) Can I stay over?

CHUMPA: Course you can, not him though.

SAB: We'll be quiet.

CHUMPA: Jesus Sab. You got protection?

SAB: No, it'll be fine.

CHUMPA: You're not getting pregnant in my mum's house.

SAB: Well you got anything then?

CHUMPA: Tut, where am I supposed to…… Wait, I'll get you something. Promise me you won't do anything before I get back?

SAB: Yes, alright Mum.

SAB and SUNIL snog.

CHUMPA runs across the street to the video shop. It is shut.

CHUMPA: Oi, open up.

MEM's voice within/offstage.

MEM: We're closed.

CHUMPA: It's an emergency.

MEM appears.

MEM: We don't get the first editions.

CHUMPA: No, not newspaper, it's personal things.

MEM: You mean women's things?

CHUMPA: I'm quite capable of saying Tampax you know.

MEM: What then?

CHUMPA: Men's things.

MEM: What kind of men's things?

CHUMPA: Jesus, what is this, twenty questions?

MEM: I wouldn't have to ask if you'd just say it.

CHUMPA: Right okay then.

She cannot quite make herself say what she wants.

MEM: Go on then.

CHUMPA: Condoms.

MEM: Sorry, what did you say? I need a packet of condoms. Alright? You realise you need a man to wear them.

CHUMPA: Really, you're very funny.

MEM: You have one then I take it?

CHUMPA: None of your bloody business. Anyone ever told you that you're really irritating?

MEM: No. Why am I?

CHUMPA: Hate to say this, but I haven't got all night.

MEM shouts towards the inside of the shop.

MEM: (*To offstage.*) It's an emergency, girl's desperate, needs some condoms.

ASHOK: Ribbed or regular? Sangeeta recommends the ribbed ones.

Male and female laughter from within.

CHUMPA: You know Sangeeta?

MEM: She's my cousin's girlfriend.

CHUMPA: Who's your cousin?

ASHOK appears with the condoms.

ASHOK: One packet of ribbed condoms.

MEM: Ashok's my cousin.

CHUMPA: Sangeeta! You bastard.

She slaps ASHOK across the face and walks off.

ASHOK: Yeah, and you're a slag. Your mother'll be hearing about this.

CHUMPA: And I suppose your father knows about Sangeeta?

MEM: I take it you two know each other?

We hear a bed squeaking and the sound of SAB being satisfied. CHUMPA throws the condoms across the stage and screams at the top of her voice.

End of Act One.

ACT TWO

Scene 1

MUM and MANOJ opening some jewellery boxes.

MANOJ: All in all about ten thousand.

The figure makes MUM anxious.

Wedding expenditure cannot be avoided, no hurry, pay me when you can.

MUM: Only a few weeks and Aunty Reno will be here with her children. Then Chachi Swaran with her son. The elders last.

MANOJ: Where is that girl?

CHUMPA enters.

CHUMPA: I suppose Ashok's told you Uncle?

MANOJ: Not uncle any more. Daddy, father, papa, not uncle. He said you had something to tell me.

CHUMPA: He didn't tell you?

MUM: What's the matter?

MANOJ: Is there a problem?

CHUMPA takes a deep breath.

CHUMPA: Mum, Uncle. Ashok and me don't want to marry each other.

MANOJ: What nonsense are you talking?

MUM: Hi, hi Chumpa.

CHUMPA: I'm sorry…

MANOJ: You can't just be sorry. You can't not marry my son. I forbid it.

CHUMPA: You can't forbid it.

MANOJ: How dare you answer me back.

MUM: Chumpa you're getting nervous that's all.

MANOJ: Do you know how much money we have invested in this marriage?

CHUMPA: Bet he didn't tell you he's been done for drink driving.

MANOJ: Bastard.

MUM: But, you can drive.

MANOJ: Of course.

CHUMPA: It's not just the driving. He doesn't love me.

MANOJ: Urray, love is a luxury, you watch too many Hindi films.

MUM: Love comes after marriage Chumpa.

CHUMPA: No Mum.

MUM is irritated.

MUM: Why did you say yes then? Nobody forced you. Why have you changed your mind?

MANOJ: Any problem we can sort out.

CHUMPA: He's seeing Sangeeta.

MUM: Sangeeta? Chaudhary's daughter?

CHUMPA: Yes.

MUM: Hi hi. What kind of son do you call that?

MANOJ: Sangeeta, that choora chamar [lowcaste toilet-cleaner] Chaudhary's choorie [lowcaste] daughter?

He paces around in a rage.

Kunjar! [bastard] I'll stop him.

MUM: We can't force them.

MANOJ: Of course we can. How are you going to pay back what you've borrowed? You are poor as it is.

MUM: Poverty is no crime. Her father said never to force her to do anything.

MANOJ: Think, what are you saying.

MUM: I am saying what I am saying.

MANOJ: Then get the accounts settled right now.

MUM: Chumpa go upstairs!

CHUMPA leaves.

MANOJ immediately begins doing some calculations on his personal organiser.

MANOJ: Ten thousand on the wedding and around six thousand on the flat. Everything was new, fridge, microwave, carpets and that doesn't include cementing the garden, the double glazing or the stone chipping.

MUM: Rent it to students.

MANOJ: What are you talking about? There's a brand new fridge, washing machine and fitted kitchen…

MUM: Sell it.

MANOJ: I have just invested another three thousand in the shop. I do not change my business plans like your daughter changes her mind.

MUM: I will pay in installments.

MANOJ: Think with a cool head, hey? If my son has done wrong, I am sorry. This is about the honour of our families. You are a woman on your own with an unmarried daughter – it is not good. What about another member of my family? After all she will have to marry somebody someday.

Scene 2

AUDREY is dictating a letter. CHUMPA is typing it.

AUDREY: '…Talk to your partner, comma, share your feelings with him, comma, and you can learn to woo each other all over again full stop.'

CHUMPA is crying as she types.

'Gradually you will find that increasing…' What's the matter?

CHUMPA: My engagement's over.

AUDREY gets a box of tissues.

AUDREY: Right, two minute blub break.

She pours out brandy into two glasses.

Men are bastards. Women get miserable. Work goes on. Can't print that unfortunately. Not what people want to hear. Knickers to the Queen.

The two toast then knock back the brandy.

The phone rings.

CHUMPA: *High Society*, hello. No, it's her assistant.

She looks across at AUDREY who shakes her head.

Vinod Kumar, yes the Bollywood actor. Fax us a press release with the details and we'll get back to you if we're interested.

CHUMPA puts the phone down.

It was that Scorpio, Vinod Kumar's agent again.

AUDREY: Oh him again, he's a real pain in the arse – always after something. What's he scamming this time?

CHUMPA: Says you can interview Vinod after the show on Thursday if you want.

AUDREY: God, if Jemima's agent doesn't ring back soon we might have to run with it. Not my first choice I have to say.

The phone rings again. CHUMPA gets it.

CHUMPA: Hello, *High Society*. No it's her assistant. Who's calling?

She covers the phone.

It's *Cosmo.*

AUDREY grabs it out of her hand.

AUDREY: Audrey Sackville. Harriet darling how are you? They do? Excellent. You just name the day. Thursday? I'll just check my diary. I'll cancel a few appointments. No, no bother at all I'd be delighted. The Ivy? Splendid. Lunch or Supper? Supper? Marvellous. See you then honey. Love to all. Bye.

(*To CHUMPA.*) Yes, yes, yes. Chumpa you've got your first break, I want you to interview that Vinod.

CHUMPA lets out an excited scream. Both are elated.

Scene 3

MUM and MANDY are at home.

MUM: She'll be happy with this one, definitely. Son of a wealthy family, has a very important job. Works with stocks and shares.

ROBIN knocks on the front door.

Haa, that must be him. Now don't panic, keep calm, he is very nice. Call her and tell her to hurry up.

She lets ROBIN in.

ROBIN: Ahh hello. We had an appointment for five, terribly sorry I'm late. Could I just have a quick word with the girl in private?

MUM: Yes, she's just getting ready.

There is a noise at the door. MUM signals to MANDY to get it. CHUMPA has arrived.

ROBIN's mobile phone goes off.

ROBIN: (*Into phone.*) Can't talk right now, I'm in an important meeting at the moment. I'll call you back.

MANDY: (*To CHUMPA.*) What kept you? Your mother's been having kittens. Put this on and get in there.

She hands her a veil and CHUMPA throws it on. MUM and ROBIN are sitting in uncomfortable silence. MANDY pushes CHUMPA into the room.

MUM: Here she is. Why don't you two get to know each other?

(*To CHUMPA under her breath.*) Be very nice to him.

She adjusts CHUMPA's veil before leaving.

ROBIN: Hi. Right, can we just get the important things out of the way. The thing is I've seen over thirty women and I've found it's best if we get down to business as quickly as possible.

He ticks the points off on his fingers.

You look fine. Now I don't expect you to be a virgin, though it would be nice. Second, how do you feel about entertaining my business guests two to three nights a week? Thirdly, I need you to think about how much money you'd need to run the household with. Living east of the city is absolutely out of the question, I've got a very nice property in Maida Vale.

CHUMPA: What's your name?

ROBIN: Oh, terribly sorry. It's Robin.

CHUMPA: What's that short for?

ROBIN: Rabinthranath.

CHUMPA: After the poet?

ROBIN: I don't know – I just know that it's terribly hard for my English colleagues to pronounce. Do you have any views about public schools? I have to let you know now that Sherborne and Uppingham are absolutely out of the question as far as I'm concerned.

His phone rings.

Yeah. Hi. I know I did. Look I'm in the middle of closing a deal. What? I'll be over right away.

He puts his phone down.

I'm afraid I've got to dash, I'm really sorry, can I call you – I'm extremely interested.

He dashes off.

MANDY and MUM appear.

MUM: So?

MANDY: What did you think?

CHUMPA: Blink and you miss him.

MUM: He's perfect.

MANDY: He's loaded, he drives a Porche.

Scene 4

VINOD is pacing up and down in a theatre dressing-room.

VINOD: I'm not doing any more stupid Indian accents for voice-overs. Haven't you noticed? Not all Indians speak with accents these days.

AGENT: Two days work and you get the repeat fees for the next three years – there's no such thing as bad publicity.

VINOD: I want Hamlet. Something to top my *Importance of Being Earnest.* 'Set in India with the traumatic backdrop of partition… Vinod Kumar's Algernon was a revelation.'

AGENT: We've had an offer for a Tilda Basmati advert. That would go some way to making you a household name. We haven't all that long to crack the crossover audience. Indians want to see you singing and dancing, not in bloody Shakespeare.

VINOD: What's happening with the work permit?

AGENT: Not so good. How's plan B coming along? It did get published didn't it?

VINOD: Yes – but where have I had the time to see anyone?

AGENT: Well you had better hurry up.

CHUMPA pops up.

CHUMPA: Hi! Hello I was wondering…

AGENT: I'm afraid Vinod's not doing any autographs at the moment.

CHUMPA: Erm, actually I've come to interview Vinod. Chumpa Chameli. *High Society.* I'm Audrey Sackville's assistant. Audrey asked me to do the profile as she's indisposed.

AGENT: Ever so sorry. You'll have to forgive me. Come in, come in.

VINOD: That's it, the interview's off. I want to talk to the organ grinder not the monkey.

CHUMPA: Hey, who you calling a monkey?

AGENT: Vinod, you're being a tad hasty. Chumpa Chameli is a fine journalist – I've enjoyed so many of her pieces.

CHUMPA: You have?

AGENT: Fine journalist.

VINOD: She is?

CHUMPA: Yeah, course I am.

The AGENT pulls up a chair.

AGENT: Take a seat. Vinod, I'll send some champagne up. Is an hour good for you Chumpa?

CHUMPA: Great.

AGENT: I'll leave you to it.

CHUMPA: I'll be recording this if you don't mind.

VINOD: Fine.

CHUMPA breaths in and collects herself.

CHUMPA: Right okay, well just the regular questions first. How old are you? How long have you been performing? What made you choose this particular career? Are you married? If not, do you hope to be? Dating anyone at the moment? And what car do you drive?

VINOD: No wife, but I'm looking. Saab Turbo. Thirty-two.

CHUMPA: You're still not married? But there were rumours about you and Raveena were there not?

VINOD: Are you a Miss or a Mrs?

CHUMPA: Miss.

VINOD: Well Miss Chameli I don't overly concern myself with rumours.

CHUMPA: So why's a dashing talented man like yourself single?

VINOD: Look. I'm not married but I hope to be one day, okay, and I hope that day is very soon. We seem to be spending a disproportionate time on this married unmarried business – I'd like to stick to questions about my career.

CHUMPA: What does the world look like through the eyes of Vinod Kumar?

VINOD: I feel that my past has been a dream, the future an illusion. I prefer to concentrate on life's simple pleasures; a really good movie, a fine bottle of wine, a starry sky with a full moon, a good cup of masala tea – the smell of jasmine in the evening air. God has been extremely kind to me and someday he will put the right woman into my path.

There is a knock at the door.

That must be the champagne.

He goes over and returns with a tray with champagne and two glasses on it.

I'm terribly sorry, it's Bollinger, tedious but sufficient. I can tell that you are the kind of lady who appreciates the finer things in life.

CHUMPA: I don't drink.

VINOD: You've never tried champagne? Why, you haven't lived. A glass surely?

CHUMPA: Okay. I was reading your list of film credits, it's impressive.

VINOD: Thank you.

He pours out the champagne and gives a glass to CHUMPA.

One should always toast.

CHUMPA: To world peace.

VINOD: No, no, to something realistic.

CHUMPA: To more good movies.

VINOD: …And Shakespeare.

CHUMPA: Shakespeare? Right.

They clink their glasses.

What greater thing is there in life but movies?

VINOD: Very little really.

CHUMPA knocks back the champagne.

CHUMPA: Hmm, this is nice.

VINOD: Sex is better than movies surely?

CHUMPA almost blurts out her champagne.

CHUMPA: Excuse me, went down the wrong way. Sex? Well, you can get that in the movies.

VINOD: Not in Indian movies you can't.

CHUMPA: And thank God for that. That's the beauty of Indian culture. It's all in the art of suggestion.

VINOD: Indian films would have us believe that women get pregnant by dipping their toes in the Ganges.

He pours more champagne.

CHUMPA: You don't need to show sex on the screen. There are lots of ways of showing two people to be in love.

She takes a huge gulp from her glass.

VINOD: There's nothing to be ashamed about with sex, it's the most natural thing in the world. It's the single most creative act known to humanity.

CHUMPA: Men will say anything to get a shag. There's a design fault with human beings. Men and women are so different it's a wonder they ever get on at all.

VINOD: We're getting on marvellously aren't we?

CHUMPA: Professionally, yes.

VINOD: Are you hungry? I'm starving, let's got out to dinner. How does Japanese sound?

The AGENT walks in.

AGENT: You nearly done? We've got a nine o'clock at thc Ritz.

VINOD: Damn! I forgot. How about Friday evening?

CHUMPA: Friday's great.

VINOD: Hilton? Savoy? You have a preference? No, no, no what am I thinking of? Just had a thought, a better idea would be to meet me on Sunday. Waterloo Station, under the clock, three p.m. I've been invited to this grand opening – you'll need your passport though.

CHUMPA: Passport?

VINOD: Let it be a surprise. Sunday then?

CHUMPA: Sunday.

VINOD takes her hand and kisses it.

VINOD: I can't tell you what a pleasure it has been meeting you. Goodbye.

He exits. CHUMPA packs her stuff and walks home.

Scene 5

MEM is looking at the enormous beautiful moon. He tries not to notice CHUMPA as she walks past.

CHUMPA: Hey, Mem, how you doing?

He pretends not to hear her.

Stop ignoring me.

MEM: Sorry?

CHUMPA: I said how you doing?

MEM: Fine. What you so happy about?

CHUMPA: I'm gonna be a writer Mem, I'm gonna have my first piece published.

MEM: You said you were a journalist.

CHUMPA: Oh yeah, but I've never interviewed a star before.

MEM: Star? What kind of star?

CHUMPA: Superstar! Bollywood.

MEM: I'm very happy for you.

He listens but is unimpressed.

CHUMPA: Don't get me wrong, I'm not star-struck – to be honest the guy's a bit of an idiot really, takes himself too seriously. He toasted to Shakespeare for God's sakes. What a twat.

She looks at MEM and registers that he's not interested.

Let's make up, be friends. I'm not as bad as you think.

MEM: Why are you always telling me what I think?

CHUMPA: Sorry about me and Ashok.

MEM: Matters of the heart are matters of the heart. There's no point taking sides.

CHUMPA: Friends then?

MEM: I'll show you some real stars, it's a great sky tonight.

CHUMPA: Is it a hobby or have you studied them?

MEM: I studied Astronomy. BA at Delhi University and PHd in Chicago.

He is suddenly really enthusiastic.

CHUMPA: So go on then talk to me of stars.

MEM: Well, they're made out of dust.

CHUMPA: But they still twinkle, twinkle.

MEM: Native Americans say that every star is a question and when they're all answered the world will end.

CHUMPA: How many answers you got?

MEM: Not many but did you know that astronomy is one of the great achievements of Indian culture?

CHUMPA: No.

MEM: My university professor was Indian.

CHUMPA: Where?

MEM: At the University of Chicago.

CHUMPA: Oh?

MEM: He won the Nobel prize for discovering that gravitational collapse is inevitable in all stars greater than one point four four times the mass of the sun. He also calculated that in smaller main sequence stars the initial gravitational collapse triggers internal electron pressure which leads to the formation of huge burned-out stars called red giants.

CHUMPA: I knew that.

MEM looks at her and realises she is joking. He smiles at her. She smiles back.

You're not thick then are you?

MEM: No. But people say I think too much.

CHUMPA: Wonder why that is. Is there life up there?

MEM: There's life everywhere.

CHUMPA looks at him in wonder.

Isn't there?

CHUMPA: I don't know – you're the expert. What sign are you? Bet you're an air sign, you're not of this planet.

MEM: You're right, Libra. And you?

CHUMPA: Cancer. Water. Water fascinates me, always find it hard to believe that there's more underneath the world then on it.

MEM: Even more in the skies. But you know where everything is?

CHUMPA: Do I look like a girl who's got all the answers?

MEM: Inside us. The human spirit. It's the best kept secret and the last place anyone thinks to look.

CHUMPA looks at him at bit gobsmacked not sure if he's nuts or not. MEM has found something interesting through the telescope.

There you go, there's Leo the lion and there's Cancer next door. I'm terrified of water.

He offers CHUMPA the telescope. They are in an intimate position and MEM does all he can not to put his arm around her as she looks through the telescope.

CHUMPA: Of water? Why?

MEM: It's a long story – it's an extreme phobia – I'd probably die if I fell into any volume of it.

CHUMPA: What? You'd die if you had a bath?

MEM: I have showers.

CHUMPA: I couldn't live without swimming – it's my only escape from the world and it's problems – you know it's the only place you can have a good cry without anyone noticing.

MEM: I just look at the moon to cheer myself up. Greece is a great place to see the stars.

CHUMPA: You've done a lot of travelling. How comes?

MEM: Dad was a stuntman and mum was a dancer. They met on a film set – we travelled around quite a bit with their work. I was actually born in Forest Gate hospital. Believe it or not this is the closest thing that comes to home. I lived in this area for the first eight years of my life. It's hard when you don't have family anchoring you.

CHUMPA: Where are they? Your parents?

MEM: Passed away.

CHUMPA: God, I'm sorry.

MEM: Dad drowned while he was doing this stunt in the river, they were filming the last scene of *Soni Mahiwal*, you know the love story where the lovers drown. A cruel joke. Avoided water ever since.

There is a silence and MEM seems to have drifted off into a daydream.

CHUMPA: God, that's awful.

MEM: Especially since three quarters of the world is water.

CHUMPA: What about brothers and sisters?

MEM: Only child.

CHUMPA: You must be so lonely.

MEM: That's why I came here – to be with family.

CHUMPA: You should get married.

MEM: I should.

CHUMPA: Why don't you?

MEM: My uncle's trying to find someone. I'm no good at relationships, I don't know how to do all that stuff. I just want someone to love for the rest of my life.

CHUMPA: Doesn't everyone?

MEM: Makes you wonder why people are so awful to each other – all in the name of love.

CHUMPA: It wasn't love.

MEM: What wasn't?

CHUMPA: Me and Ashok.

MEM: No… I didn't mean you…

There is a pause.

It wasn't?

CHUMPA: No.

Another pause.

I better go.

MEM: Wait. Have you seen *Cinema Paradiso*?

CHUMPA: No.

MEM: Take this.

He gives her a video-tape.

It's my own copy. You won't get charged for the fines.

CHUMPA: This may sound like a stupid question but I sometimes dream whole films in my sleep. Do you?

MEM: Of course – with the credits.

CHUMPA: Jesus, I thought I had problems. I had better go before you do my head in completely.

MEM: It's been nice talking to you. Tell me if you like the film.

CHUMPA: Okay. See ya.

She makes her way through the shop and MEM looks on.

CHUMPA walks home still humming to herself. She enters the house and listens to what's going on.

MANOJ: Touch your mother-in-law's feet and beg for forgiveness.

ASHOK: I ain't touching no one's feet. Look I'm sorry Aunty for drink driving.

MANOJ: What about Sangeeta?

ASHOK: Look Dad, Chumpa don't want to marry me, if she did she would have said something.

MANOJ: Shut up!

MUM: There's no point.

MANOJ: Point? Point? There is every point, for our community, for our families. For the love of our children. You marry her into another family and you have no surety how they will treat her. With Ashok she is across the road. What will become of you if she leaves the area? You going to sit at home all day watching Zee TV with no one to love? Hey? What about your grandchildren? If she marries away in Leeds, Glasgow, India, who is to say that you will ever see them?

ASHOK's mobile rings and MANOJ grabs it off of him.

(*Into phone.*) Hello? Sangeeta? You leave my son alone, otherwise I'll break your legs.

ASHOK goes to grab the phone from MANOJ. They push and shove but MANOJ keeps hold of it.

ASHOK: That's my phone, man.

MANOJ: (*Into phone.*) Does your Dad know hey? I'll tell him myself, ruining my family… What the bloody hell you think you're playing at? We are Indians, not bloody angreaj [white people], and cover yourself up wearing mini skirts like that…

He has the phone put down on him.

ASHOK: You're bang out of order Dad! You can't go round treating everyone the way you treat me. Sangeeta's done nothing wrong and nor have I! You're nothing but a big fat bully! This flippin' marriage business is nothing but a bloody farce.

He storms out and MANOJ takes his shoe off and chucks it at him but it fails to hit him. ASHOK bumps into CHUMPA and stares at her with hate in his eyes.

You keep away from me and my family, right.

He makes a point of bumping his shoulder into her as he walks past her. CHUMPA continues to listen to MANOJ and MUM's conversation.

MUM is putting all the gold jewellery into cases and attempting to give it back to MANOJ.

MUM: Take these – they do not belong here.

MANOJ: Why you shaming me, hey?

MUM: Please.

MANOJ: We must make our hearts big. Keep them for a few days, give me that much time to sort things out, if I can't there will be no mention of the wedding ever again.

MUM nods a small reluctant nod.

I will call.

And with that MANOJ leaves. CHUMPA makes sure he doesn't see her. MUM in the meantime is sitting crying, CHUMPA hears her.

MUM looks to the heavens.

MUM: If you were alive now, she would listen to you. Left me alone – who can I turn to? No one to wipe a widow's tears. Give me guidance. Help me please, help me.

CHUMPA walks in and puts her arm around her MUM. She looks at all the jewels on the table.

CHUMPA: Mum, don't cry, not over me, please.

MUM continues to cry.

Mum, I'm not going to marry Ashok.

MUM cries louder.

I'll marry Robin.

MUM is stunned. She blows her nose and wipes her tears.

MUM: Robin? You will beti?

CHUMPA: Yes mum.

MUM: Definitely? A hundred per cent.

CHUMPA: Two hundred per cent.

MUM: Oh, Chumpa.

She hugs CHUMPA. We hear some light wedding music overhead for a while.

Scene 6

MEM and ASHOK walk across the stage.

ASHOK: Come on hurry up, Jagi's waiting down The Queen's Head. Oh, and Dad said he wants to see you tomorrow. Family business.

MEM: Right.

Scene 7

In the changing rooms. CHUMPA is sobbing away and MANDY is trying to appease her. SAB enters.

SAB: What's going on?

MANDY: Robin said no.

SAB: No!

MANDY: Don't know what she's crying about it. The guy's a wanker, nice Porche though.

SAB: Why?

MANDY: Why's he a wanker?

SAB: No why's he say no?

MANDY: Cos he's a wanker I suppose.

SAB: Come on Chumps.

CHUMPA: Nobody wants to marry me. What's wrong with me?

MANDY: You can't take things personally.

CHUMPA: Ashok didn't want to marry me because he loves Sangeeta and now Robin doesn't want to marry me, because, because, said I was 'unsuitable'. I'm unmarriable, nobody's every going to marry me.

She cries harder.

MANDY: You're being ridiculous and self-indulgent. Snap out of it.

SAB: Have a good cry and get it out of your system. What about that guy from India? Your aunt with the moustache suggested him.

MANDY: The divorced guy?

SAB: I thought his first wife died?

MANDY: Yeah, strangled by her sari in the wheels of a rickshaw, allegedly.

SAB: A suspected murderer – we're not that desperate.

MANDY: Yet.

CHUMPA sobs louder.

SAB: Did you like this Robin geezer?

CHUMPA: No.

SAB: (*To MANDY.*) Why she crying then?

MANDY: It's rejection isn't it.

SAB: Oh yeah.

MANDY: Come on Chumps pull yourself together. Your mum sent more photos – have a look at this lot and see if you like anyone.

SAB and MANDY flick through some photographs of some men and make horrified faces.

CHUMPA cries harder when she sees how bad the men are.

Scene 8

In a gurdwara [sikh temple] a shabad [hymn] plays overhead. CHUMPA and MUM have their head covered.

CHUMPA: Look God, we've got three weeks – find someone, anyone, how hard can it be to find a bloke? I mean you're supposed to perform miracles, allegedly. I'm not asking for Mr Perfect – just a decent bloke. Emotionally and financially responsible, no criminal record, sense of humour, generous, artistic, doesn't have to be really handsome, I mean not pig ugly obviously. No major vice, not violent, a liar or thick, gotta be able to dance. You know, just a nice guy.

MUM: Say yes to this one.

CHUMPA: Can I at least see him first. I said yes to Robin and look what happened?

MUM: Your grandparents will be arriving on Friday. Please save me shame.

CHUMPA: If he's a nice guy I'll say yes.

MUM: I am your mother, I worry about you more than you worry about yourself, you think I would show you someone less than perfect? It is your happiness that we are searching for.

CHUMPA: Alright. But why we meeting him at the temple?

MUM: It is the way his family wanted it. He's very well-educated, has a PHd. A lovely boy, hard-working, honest. He's from India.

CHUMPA: I said no MFIs!

MUM: What's an MFI?

CHUMPA: Man From India.

MUM: You might like him. Consider things with a cool head, I'll get him.

CHUMPA: Hurry up I've got to get to work.

MUM: On Sunday?

CHUMPA: Got to meet this idiot for something.

MUM exits. CHUMPA waits.

MEM walks in feeling a bit self conscious. CHUMPA looks at him and is a bit taken aback. MEM looks uncomfortable.

Oh, hi. Didn't think you were the religious sort?

MEM: Hi. I'm more spiritual than religious.

CHUMPA: So what you doing here?

MEM: Come to see someone.

CHUMPA: Who?

MEM: A girl. And you?

CHUMPA: Got a meeting too.

They both stand there in uncomfortable silence for a while not quite sure what is going on.

I hope you don't mind me asking but what you meeting her for exactly?

MEM: Ashok's dad's finally found someone suitable. She's supposed to be clever, funny, good-looking. Sounds hopeful.

CHUMPA: Oh I get it. That's called taking the piss big time. You Sahota's are disgusting.

MEM: Sorry?

CHUMPA: You devious crafty snake. What does your uncle think I am, some off-the-shelf company that he can pass from one member of the family to another?

MEM: Hey, hold on a minute. What makes you think I knew it was you? I wouldn't have bothered coming had I known.

CHUMPA: What? Why? What's wrong with me?

MEM: Where do I start. I mean, you spent seven years with Ashok without realising that you were wrong for each other. You've got a foul mouth. You're stroppy, confrontational, cold and as far as I can tell emotionally constipated. Exactly what makes you think you're such a great catch?

CHUMPA: Listen Oracle of Delphi. I don't have to listen to your crap. You can tell your uncle that whatever happens I won't be marrying into his crappy family. Got it? I thought you were my sodding friend.

She storms out.

MEM: You're not supposed to swear in the house of God.

CHUMPA: (*Shouting back.*) Oh, go to hell.

(*Alone.*) Look God, I don't know what you're playing at but I think you're taking the piss. I want a husband who's talented, kind and nothing to do with the Sahota family, you hear me? I'll give you twenty-four hours otherwise I'll assume you don't exist.

She walks on in a huff.

Waterloo Station, under the clock. CHUMPA stands by, waiting, looking at her watch impatiently. VINOD strolls on.

VINOD: Hi, thank you for that wonderful piece.

CHUMPA: That's alright, it's my job. Now what did you want?

VINOD: Oh, I was hoping you like French food?

CHUMPA: Suppose. Why?

VINOD: You did bring your passport didn't you?

CHUMPA: As instructed.

VINOD: We're off to Paris, we've got first class tickets on Eurostar, there's an opening at The Louvre and then we'll have dinner at The Ritz there. How's that sound?

CHUMPA: Paris! Great, let's go.

She gets her passport out.

No, don't look at the picture.

He looks at her picture and laughs. She snatches at his passport and tries to get it from him. He holds it above her head and they have a mock fight as they walk.

Let's see yours then.

VINOD: I look like a serial killer.

A romantic tune plays overhead. They are in Paris. They sit at a table having a lavish meal. A waiter keeps the alcohol flowing.

I wouldn't mind getting married if I could find the right kind of woman.

CHUMPA: I'm having the same problem with men. What would she be like?

VINOD: She'd have to understand me, let me live my life the way I want to.

CHUMPA: Sounds reasonable enough.

VINOD: To have a western outlook – be broad-minded about things.

CHUMPA: And what would you offer them in return?

VINOD: My name, my money, my company. I'd like to get married soon. If I found the right girl I wouldn't waste time. I mean once you've found the right person, what's there to wait for?

CHUMPA: That's to assume you'd find them.

VINOD: That's a terribly sad thing to say. Why wouldn't you?

CHUMPA: Not everyone does do they?

VINOD: Who cares about everyone – I'm talking about us.

CHUMPA: Us?

VINOD: You might be a good person to marry.

CHUMPA: I know a lot of boys who would disagree with that.

VINOD: That's ridiculous, I'm surprised you weren't married years ago. Must be destiny.

CHUMPA: What?

VINOD: Look, I haven't stopped thinking about you since our last meeting. I thought that maybe all that charm of yours was just a journalistic ploy and then I read your interview and what shone out at me was your sincerity. You have a pure heart and that is rare. I don't know how to say this, it may seem a bit forward but you see I'm a busy man which makes me appreciate time, of others and my own. And I certainly know that time waits for no man. Chumpa, God chose that I be an artist and artists do not always do what is right in the eyes of convention. I don't have long in this country – perhaps only a week or two and then who knows where work will take me. I've met a lot of girls in my life, many whom would fall at my feet at the drop of a hat which does not flatter me it appals me that they are so shallow. I mean they don't know who I am, they don't know the real Vinod, all they know is the celluloid dream, which is all a lie. I need a strong woman, a committed woman, one with character and ability. I know this is only our second meeting but my search for a partner has been long and tough but I have been patient. And finally, finally Chumpa it would seem that God has answered my prayers. I don't assume you feel the same way – everyone knows unrequited love is around every corner. I have to go back to India soon but before I make arrangements I would like you to think about something, about, about the possibility of us having a future together Chumpa.

CHUMPA is speechless. She is about to utter something. VINOD puts his finger on her lips.

Don't say anything tonight. Think about it. I'll call you tomorrow. Goodnight.

He strokes her cheek with his finger tenderly and exits.

CHUMPA is back at home outside her house, she hums to herself. She is happy, floating on air. MEM is about to lock up the shop. He watches CHUMPA for a while, she notices him and gives him a big smile.

CHUMPA: I'm so happy that I can't even be bothered not to talk to you.

MEM: I'm honoured.

CHUMPA: There is a god and he's great and wonderful and he answers all of our prayers, eventually.

MEM: Really?

CHUMPA: Yes and he forgives us everything.

MEM: How's that?

CHUMPA: I'm in love Mem, in love.

MEM: You are? What, in love like when Hema meets Dharmender in *Sholay*?

CHUMPA: Like when Raj Kumar meets Meena Kumari asleep on the train in *Pakeezah*.

MEM: Like when Woody meets Diane in *Annie Hall*?

CHUMPA: Like when Katherine Hepburn meets Jimmy Stewart in *The Philadelphia Story*.

MEM: Cary Grant you mean. She doesn't end up with Jimmy. Don't you remember the twist at the end?

CHUMPA: Oh, yeah, but who cares. Love is love and I'm in it.

MEM: I know you are.

CHUMPA: Is it in my eyes?

MEM: Let's take a closer look.

CHUMPA stares at him and lets him look into her eyes. They get locked in a gaze for a while. Until CHUMPA snaps herself out of it.

Your eyes are…

CHUMPA: I know…the window to your soul.

MEM: Liver.

CHUMPA: What?

MEM: According to Chinese medicine that is.

CHUMPA: God you haven't got a romantic bone in your body.

MEM: And your eyes tell me you've had too much to drink. It's easy to think you're in love when you're drunk.

CHUMPA: I am not drunk. You can smell my breath.

She gets up close to him and opens her mouth to breathe onto his face. It seems as if she is about to kiss him but MEM breaks out of it.

MEM: You are drunk. I think you better go home.

They stand facing each other.

CHUMPA: I'm sorry for the things I said. I know you didn't really want to marry me – did you?

MEM: You're in love.

CHUMPA: I am.

They look into each other's eyes for a while.

Scene 9

The AGENT and VINOD.

AGENT: We agreed, plan B was your responsibility.

VINOD: I said I'm working on it.

AGENT: Well Hamlet, won't be there forever. They'll look elsewhere. Get someone from here. God knows it would be a whole lot easier.

VINOD: Panic is really unattractive.

AGENT: Well hurry up and do something. I can only stall them for so long.

VINOD: Have I ever let you down?

AGENT: There's a first time for everything.

Scene 10

CHUMPA is working away furiously at her desk. AUDREY is putting her coat on.

AUDREY: I'll only be away a couple of weeks. Any emergencies just e-mail me. I'll be picking up. I've got to dash – cab's waiting. Barbados here I come. See you.

She blows her kiss.

CHUMPA: Have a wonderful time.

AUDREY exits. CHUMPA is overwhelmed and sighs.

VINOD walks in carrying flowers. He walks over to CHUMPA's desk and puts his hand over her eyes.

Vinod.

VINOD: How did you know?

CHUMPA: I hoped.

VINOD: For you.

CHUMPA: Ahh.

VINOD: I couldn't sleep last night. It's as if I'm floating on air. I can't stop thinking about you.

CHUMPA: I've been feeling the same way too.

VINOD: Do you have to work? Can't we go someplace? I feel like celebrating, dancing.

CHUMPA: Let's go!

VINOD: Someplace special.

CHUMPA: Very special.

> *VINOD takes her by the hand and there is a dance number in which the world lights up. VINOD and CHUMPA fall in love.*

VINOD: Chumpa I love you. Will you marry me?

CHUMPA: I'd love to.

Scene 11

CHUMPA's MUM is fussing around the house. Things seem hectic.

MUM is on the phone and pretending that the phone line has a fault.

MUM: Jeetho! No there is no problem the wedding is going ahead. He is a lovely boy. His name? His name? Hello? Hello? The line has gone bad. Jeetho? I will call you back. I can't hear you. Goodbye.

> *CHUMPA and VINOD are walking arm in arm down the street.*

VINOD: The urgency is professional. You realise that?

CHUMPA: Of course I do. It's not a problem. I prefer it this way, honest.

VINOD: What will your mum think? She'll think it suspicious, only known him a short while and already……

> *CHUMPA puts her finger on his lips to make him be quiet and then kisses him.*

CHUMPA: It hasn't been a short while. It's as if we've known you all our lives. Mum loves your movies.

VINOD: I hope she isn't expecting too much.

CHUMPA: Don't worry. She'll want to know why you always play the villain though. Don't you ever want the romantic lead?

VINOD: Only in my own life. Indian cinema-goers hate you to be different from what you were in previous films. Heroes are heroes and villains are villains, forever. That's why I want to work in the west, people don't come with the same narrow-minded expectations. I'm so nervous, this is worse than stage fright.

CHUMPA: Relax, you'll be fine.

They go into the house.

Mum, this is Vinod.

MUM: Hello beta [son]. Sit, sit. Tea?

VINOD: No thank you. I'll get straight to the point Mrs Chameli. If my parents were here they would have come themselves to ask you but they are in India so I have to break with tradition. Mrs Chameli I would like to marry your daughter if you will let me.

MUM: It would be an honour son to have you in our family. What a blessing. I'm so happy.

She bursts into tears.

CHUMPA is grinning ear to ear.

CHUMPA: Come on Mum. Don't cry.

VINOD offers her a red silk handkerchief to wipe her tears.

VINOD: Money is no object and I don't believe in dowries. All that matters is that people enjoy themselves on the day. Is that okay?

MUM: Beta you are like a god – too kind. A perfect son, Chumpa your destiny is beautiful. I'll get us some tea. Thank you son. Thank you.

She starts dialling the phone immediately. VINOD and CHUMPA kiss.

(*Into phone.*) Jeetho, can you hear me? His name is Vinod Kumar. Yes, yes the actor. You come on the next flight yes. Tell everyone. My daughter is marrying a Bollywood film star.

Music.

Scene 12

CHUMPA goes to see MANOJ.

MANOJ: So you've changed your mind?

CHUMPA takes out three bundles of cash from her bag.

CHUMPA: No. Here's the money we owe you so stop bothering my mum and making her feel bad.

MANOJ: I'm not making anyone feel bad. It's you. Your problem? You have no faith, lost and confused.

CHUMPA: Is that right?

MANOJ: We were the same when we first came to this country, but life teaches you. You remind me of myself, think things will only happen if you make them. You should trust life a bit more, it does what it wants to do – let it into your heart.

CHUMPA: I'm marrying Vinod with or without your blessing.

MANOJ: Vinod, that cheap film star! Chumpa actors are puppets, they care little of others, only of their next role and their egos. It is the nature of their work. All flash no substance. A girl of your intelligence been taken in by him?

CHUMPA: I'm off.

MANOJ: The stars say that you will marry into my family, guruji said.

CHUMPA: I'm marrying a star of my own.

MANOJ: We may never have seen eye to eye but I always admired you. The greatest compliment a man can pay a girl is to ask her to join his family.

CHUMPA: Thanks for the compliment.

She goes to leave.

MANOJ: In that case, I want nothing more to do with your family – take this money from my desk.

CHUMPA: It's yours.

MANOJ: I want nothing from you. Not even your money.

CHUMPA does not move for a moment.

I said take it! And get out!

CHUMPA takes the money and leaves. She is obviously shaken up. She makes her way to the video shop.

Scene 13

Inside the video shop.

CHUMPA: You coming to my hen night tonight?

MEM: No. I'm not.

CHUMPA: Why on earth not?

MEM: There's an eclipse tonight.

CHUMPA: What!? You'd rather stay in and watch a boring eclipse. Is it a total eclipse or something?

MEM: Even a partial eclipse is better than your stupid hen night.

CHUMPA: It's not stupid. What's so great about a piece of rock with the light off anyway?

MEM: The moon is two thousand, one hundred and sixty miles in diameter and four point five billion years old. e.e cummings thought it was a balloon – it's been a symbol of romantic love since time immemorial. But you wouldn't know that because you're the most unromantic person I've ever met.

CHUMPA: What?

MEM: You shopped around for love as if you were buying a fridge freezer or something.

CHUMPA: Vinod's not a fridge.

MEM: No you're right. You are.

CHUMPA: Why you giving me such a hard time?

MEM: You've only known him five minutes.

CHUMPA: So? What you getting bent out of shape about?

MEM: Some of us have feelings.

CHUMPA: Hey, listen, stargazer – I got plenty of feelings.

MEM: Well you hide them pretty well.

CHUMPA: What the hell is that supposed to mean?

MEM: What feelings? Where are they? You're so passionate about so much and so fickle with relationships. Why on earth are you marrying that, that, Vinod? Have you no faith that the right guy is out there?

CHUMPA: Listen Mr Moping Visionary, PHd in bollocks. There's all sorts of love and I ain't getting any younger. I want to get married so that my mum can see me wed. I want my kids to be held by their grandmother. The right guy may or may not be out there – I certainly haven't found him in twenty-eight years and there's no guarantees that I ever will. All this love nonsense keeps us stupid, dissatisfied. I mean have you actually seen what's out there? Cos you know what? It ain't great, it ain't the movies. It's shit. I've spent so long worrying about my marriage that I want it over and done with, get on with life and get the hell out of this place. And you know what? Don't bother coming tonight because I bet you're a crap dancer anyway.

SAB and MANDY barge in.

SAB: Told you she'd be here. Oi! Gasbag, we've been waiting ages.

MANDY: Selfridges' shoe department right now. I want to be tangoing in red heels.

SAB: (*To CHUMPA.*) You alright?

CHUMPA: Fine, let's get going.

She takes a video-tape out of her bag.

(*To MEM.*) And here's your stupid *Cinema Paradiso.*

MEM: You didn't like it?

CHUMPA: I hated it.

MANDY: Oh how could you? It's a fantastic film.

CHUMPA: Oh shut up.

She storms off.

MANDY does a bit of a double take.

SAB: There's definitely something wrong if you don't like *Cinema Paradiso.* Must be because she's getting married, does strange things to you marriage. Are you married?

MEM: No.

MANDY: I'm sure we can fix that – come to the ball tonight – it's only down the road, it's gonna be a laugh.

SAB: Are you the weird one she keeps talking about?

MANDY: (*To MEM.*) Ignore her, she's mad. Seeya tonight.

They leave in an excited state. MEM looks after CHUMPA.

Outside the video shop.

What was that all about? You've got a face like a Rottweiler's arse.

CHUMPA: I've got a lot on my mind.

SAB: Like what?

CHUMPA: Like wondering how we're gonna spend all this money.

She gets the bundles of money that ASHOK's father refused to take from her earlier.

SAB: Jesus Christ Chumps where did you get it?

CHUMPA: Vinod.

MANDY: Vinod was definitely the right choice.

SAB: What a guy. Worth all the trouble.

CHUMPA: Let's shop.

MANDY/SAB: Let's.

MANDY and SAB smell the money and throw it in the air.

A shopping sequence to music follows. All three girls try on the most beautiful clothes and choose their outfits for the Salsa ball.

Scene 14

ASHOK and MEM are in the video shop passing a joint between them and getting stoned.

ASHOK: Stay for a few months. What you gonna do in America? You can run the shop since you love it so much.

MEM: Nah, I came for your wedding and your dad can't find me a girl. What's the point?

ASHOK: You don't have to go tomorrow though.

MEM: I'll balance the books before I go, make sure everything's in order.

ASHOK: She's marrying an actor – probably a poof. Dad told me that he tried to fix you two up.

MEM: Oh. I did it as a family favour.

ASHOK: Is that why you're leaving?

MEM: Don't be stupid.

ASHOK: She would have been better off with you than with that muppet.

MEM: Well she's on her hen night tonight. She's a pain in the arse, like you said.

ASHOK: You don't mean that – this drug here man is a lie detector. With these herbs man has reasoned with the gods.

MEM: Don't. I'm zoned out already.

ASHOK: I'm pretty mashed as well.

MEM: Better roll another one then.

ASHOK: Good man.

MEM: What about Sangeeta? You going to marry her?

ASHOK: I ain't marrying Sangeeta. Ain't ready to marry no one. Not for a long time. Life ain't simple.

MEM: 'Life is difficult.' The Buddha said it himself, and if it was difficult for him…

ASHOK: Respect.

Scene 15

The Salsa Ball has begun and things are beginning to warm up.

SAB: Check what's just walked in?

MEM enters looking stunning. He is not entirely sober. He grabs SAB's arm and twirls her into himself.

You're a fantastic dancer.

MEM: Thank you.

MANDY: Wow, he's great. What's his name?

CHUMPA acts as if she doesn't know who MEM is.

CHUMPA: Who?

MANDY: The video shop guy?

CHUMPA: Who? Oh, him, Mem.

MANDY: I'm going to ask him for a dance.

CHUMPA: No don't.

MANDY: Why?

CHUMPA: Isn't it supposed to be the other way around? They're supposed to ask you, the men.

MANDY: You're so last century.

She walks off and leaves CHUMPA standing self-consciously on her own. She pretends not to be the slightest bit interested in MEM. MEM twirls SAB away and then MANDY towards him – the three are having a great time. VINOD makes an entrance and CHUMPA is relieved that he has arrived. She kisses him enthusiastically. VINOD takes a good look around the joint to assess any opposition.

VINOD: Sorry I'm late darling – the Hamlet audition was intense and lasted forever.

CHUMPA: How did it go?

VINOD: Hard to say, I can never tell with auditions. They'll let us know in the morning. Who's Travolta?

CHUMPA: Oh he's the idiot from the video shop.

VINOD: Is something the matter?

CHUMPA: No nothing, let's dance.

VINOD: Let's.

A competitive dance number starts with MEM, SAB and MANDY trying to out-dance VINOD and CHUMPA. At one point in the dance MEM accidentally ends up with CHUMPA in his arms – the two dance in such a way that shows all the pent up sexual tension that exists between them.

CHUMPA: (*To VINOD.*) I want to go home.

VINOD: Already?

CHUMPA: I don't feel to good.

VINOD: I'll get your coat.

SAB comes up to CHUMPA all excited.

SAB: He's gorgeous.

CHUMPA: I know, that's why I'm marrying him.

SAB: I meant Mem not Vinod. He's such a sweetie. He's off to America tomorrow, can't you get him to stay for your wedding?

CHUMPA: Why?

SAB: I thought he was your mate.

CHUMPA: Was.

SAB: Why what happened?

CHUMPA: I'm going home, I don't feel well.

SAB: I'll pop around later.

CHUMPA: No don't. Mum'll be asleep.

SAB: See you first thing then. Chumps you're getting married tomorrow!

She gives CHUMPA an excited hug.

I'm so happy – I'm gonna snog Mem.

CHUMPA rolls her eyes. VINOD comes over and offers CHUMPA his arm. She hooks her own into his. He walks her home.

CHUMPA: Tomorrow's the day then.

VINOD: Finally. I've been looking forward to it all my life.

CHUMPA: All your life?

VINOD: It's Hamlet.

CHUMPA: I meant the wedding.

VINOD: Oh, God, I'm so sorry, it's been a really exhausting day. I'm just hoping I'll get the part so that at least we'll be settled for a while after the wedding. I'd hate to be apart from you. Chumpa, you have no idea how dear you are to me.

He holds her face in his hands and looks at her lovingly.

CHUMPA: More or less than Hamlet?

VINOD: I wouldn't be able to do Hamlet without you. You're my inspiration.

CHUMPA: Honestly?

VINOD: That's the absolute truth. I can't wait to marry you. Tonight's going to be the longest night.

CHUMPA forces a smile. VINOD gives her a tender kiss.

Goodnight darling.

CHUMPA: Goodnight.

VINOD walks off and CHUMPA looks at the stars.

God, Branson was right, life does what it wants – there's just no knowing what's around the corner. Getting married tomorrow. It's what I wanted, wasn't it? Yeah, everything's great. Just one last thing though God, could Vinod get the part of Hamlet please? It would help both of us.

She hears some giggling. MEM and SAB are staggering home arm in arm having a drunken conversation.

SAB: Oh, don't go tomorrow, please, please, pretty please. What's in America anyway?

MEM: Oh, Carnegie Hall, Broadway, Hollywood……

SAB: No I meant – is there someone special in your life?

MEM: There appears to be doesn't there?

SAB takes this to mean her.

SAB: Can I stay over?

She then goes to kiss him. CHUMPA doesn't know what to do with herself.

CHUMPA: Sab! Sab!

SAB: What you doing up?

CHUMPA: Couldn't sleep. You're my bridesmaid and you're staying over – use the back door.

SAB: I thought you said…?

CHUMPA: Back door, now!

SAB gives MEM a peck on the cheek.

SAB: (*To MEM.*) I better go, she acts like my mother. Don't go without saying goodbye tomorrow. Thanks for a great night.

CHUMPA: Anytime today.

SAB exits and CHUMPA and MEM stand there looking at each other in the hope one or the other will say something. Neither seems to for a while.

MEM: There's a lot of things I didn't say.

SAB: Chumpa! Quick get me a bucket I'm gonna be sick.

CHUMPA: Shhhhhhh!

She exits to help SAB. MEM sways out of sight. We hear SAB throwing up. CHUMPA reappears and can't see MEM.

Mem! Mem!

MEM sways back into vision and CHUMPA calms herself.

What things didn't you say?

MEM: Oh, lots of things. Anyway, what does it matter? I'm off to America tomorrow. So? Congratulations.

He puts his hand out to shake CHUMPA's hand and they continue to shake hands as they speak.

CHUMPA: Right…thanks…

MEM: So I guess this is goodbye.

CHUMPA: Suppose it is.

> *MEM tries to get his hand back, CHUMPA can't seem to let go of it.*

MEM: I'll be off then.

> *CHUMPA is getting anxious at the thought of him going.*

CHUMPA: Right, erm…you know what? You have to kiss the bride. Everyone does. It's a tradition. If you don't we both get bad luck.

MEM: Right.

> *He goes to kiss one of her cheeks – there's a bit of confusion as to which cheek when CHUMPA takes the initiative and kisses MEM on the lips – they enjoy a long passionate kiss. MEM holds CHUMPA's face in his hands.*

Let me ask you something.

CHUMPA: What?

MEM: Did you really hate *Cinema Paradiso*?

CHUMPA: No. I loved it.

> *The two of them stand looking into each other's eyes.*

MEM: It's gonna to be hard to forget you Chumpa. Goodbye.

> *CHUMPA can't seem to bring herself to say goodbye. MEM walks off and CHUMPA watches him, she is close to tears. She stays up all night thinking, watching the stars as night turns to day.*

Scene 16

Wedding activity is beginning in the house. Wedding music plays loudly. MUM is pacing around anxious. MANOJ is trying to appease her.

MUM: I tell you she was here fully dressed as a bride. Gone without saying anything. I can't take it. Don't know what bad planets gave me such a daughter.

MANOJ: Keep calm, your heart is not good. These are bad omens.

A mobile phone rings.

MUM: Mandy? You find my daughter right now otherwise I'll break your legs as well.

She puts the phone down. It rings again.

Sab where is Chumpa? You find her right now otherwise I'll burn this house bloody house down.

MANOJ: Guruji said that she should marry into my family. Listen we'll find her and then her and Ashok can get married. I'll speak to him.

He starts dialling his mobile phone and leaves.

MUM starts to wail, beating her chest with her hands.

MUM: Hey bhagwan [God] this is my family's ruin. What kind of daughter have you cursed me with?

AUDREY arrives.

AUDREY: My God, everything alright?

MUM quickly composes herself.

MUM: It's just an Indian tradition sit. Mother is sad that daughter is going. You can join me.

They are both wailing and beating their chests.

Scene 17

VINOD is holding a skull in his hand. The AGENT is pacing around him.

VINOD: 'To be, or not to be, – that is the question: – Whether 'tis nobler in the mind to suffer the slings and arrows of outrageous fortune, or to take arms against a sea of troubles…'

AGENT: Will you stop that. You've got the part now let's get the passport. Get the formalities over with and then we'll celebrate properly.

VINOD: 'Be thy intents wicked or charitable, thou com'st in such a questionable shape…'

AGENT: You've got four weeks of rehearsals, now get that garland on.

VINOD: I really wish I didn't have to marry that stupid girl.

AGENT: Everything has a price, especially Hamlet at The National. Let's go.

VINOD puts his garland on and makes his way to MUM's.

Scene 18

MEM is about to leave for his travels.

MEM: That's everything. Chumpa's still got a couple of overdue tapes.

ASHOK: Well you better go over there and get 'em from her.

MEM: Don't be ridiculous. On her wedding day?

ASHOK: Yeah, business is business.

His mobile phone goes off.

Dad. What? Chumpa? Where is she? Don't be out of order, I'm not marrying her. Well no one's gonna marry her if they can't find her. I'll go over to Aunty's now.

(*To MEM.*) Family disaster. Let's go.

Scene 19

A garlanded VINOD is now shouting at MUM.

VINOD: Mrs Chameli I demand to see Chumpa now. This marriage was supposed to happen hours ago, now I'm running out of patience and nobody keeps Vinod Kumar waiting.

AUDREY: Vinod Kumar? The actor? What you doing here?

VINOD: I'm the groom.

AUDREY: What? I thought she was marrying her silly boyfriend Ashok.

ASHOK: Oi! That's me if you don't mind.

AUDREY: Well if I were you I should jolly well do something about this. I know for a fact that this man is only marrying her for a passport, needed it for Hamlet. His agent Scorpio's been asking anyone and everyone for a marriage of convenience. Stupid, stupid Chumpa, I warned her.

ASHOK: Hamlet? Well nice to meet you Hamlet.

He puts his hand out to shake VINOD's and then punches him in the face.

VINOD: No! Not the face.

MUM slaps ASHOK.

MUM: Ashok what have you done to him? You've killed my son-in-law. Hi, hi, God what is going on? Anyone, someone find my daughter and get her married, my heart can't take it.

AUDREY: Calm down Ms Chameli.

MUM: Ashok you marry her, what about you Mem? Anyone! Someone please marry my daughter!

She suddenly gets breathless and collapses.

AUDREY: Someone call an ambulance.

The sound of thunder. MEM puts his hand out to see if it's raining.

MEM: Water…

Scene 20

CHUMPA is sobbing in the changing rooms taking her wedding sari off.

CHUMPA: It all happened so quickly God. I promised because I thought Mum was dying and now she'll probably die of shame. I don't know what to do any more God, I really don't.

She sobs. She finishes taking her wedding outfit off.

My life's been one big joke – there's only one decent thing to do.

She jumps into the deep end of the swimming pool – we are to assume that she has every intention of drowning herself.

MEM comes running in.

MEM: Chumpa! Everyone's waiting.

CHUMPA resurfaces.

CHUMPA: I thought you'd gone?

MEM is out of breath.

MEM: Those things I didn't say? Well that day at the temple I didn't know I was meeting you – when I saw you I was over the moon. I liked you before I ever knew about you and Ashok. And it doesn't matter that Ashok's my cousin because if he wasn't I'd never have met you. I've been waiting to meet you all my life. You drive me nuts Chumpa, you're infuriating and I want to spend the rest of my life arguing with you. I mean life without you would be like Clint Eastwood without his cigar, a sky without a moon, a swimming pool without water. I love you like Soni loved Mahiwal. I love you Chumpa!

And with that declaration he jumps into the pool. Splash!

CHUMPA: Mem, you can't swim!

Blackout.

MEM is lying drenched at the side of the swimming pool while CHUMPA is desperately attempting to resuscitate him. She talks to God as she does so.

Oh, God, don't let him die, please don't. I finally find the man I love and he's dead. Please let him live. Mem you can't die. I'll get married, I promise I will. Honest God. Not because of Mum or what people say or anything – because, because he's my soul-mate.

She cries into MEM's chest.

God knows that I love you Mem, God knows.

MEM splutters and opens his eyes.

MEM: You'll marry me?

CHUMPA: No. You're marrying me.

The two snog and Indian-coloured confetti falls from the sky. Bhangra music plays.

The End.